T0381328

ISBN
978-1-4828-9685-5 (sc)
978-1-4828-2895-5 (e)

Print information available on the last page.

To order additional copies of this book, contact
Toll Free 800 101 2657 (Singapore)
Toll Free 1 800 81 7340 (Malaysia)
www.partridgepublishing.com/singapore
orders.singapore@partridgepublishing.com

02/10/2015

PARTRIDGE

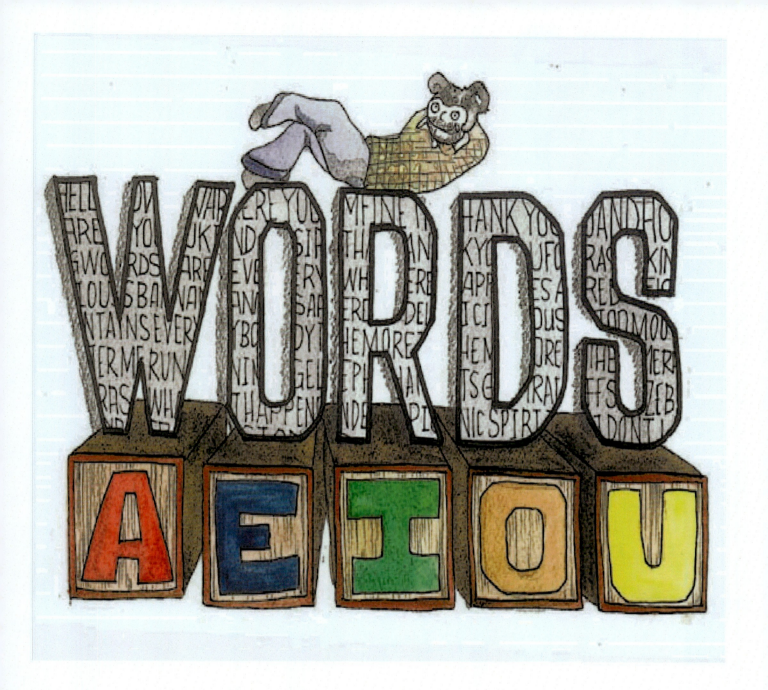

A, E, I, O, U are the five vowels that are found in almost every word.

'**A**' is for '**a**ll' of our family and friends, including you and me.

Big 'A' is tall with a point, two long legs and a belt at the knees.

Little 'a' is short with a round belly and flat back.

The vowel 'a' is in the word "say".

'**E**' is for '**e**v**e**ryon**e**', meaning all of us and others too.

Big 'E' is tall and straight with three arms.

Little 'e' is short with a round head sitting on its tail.

The vowel 'e' is in the word "hello".

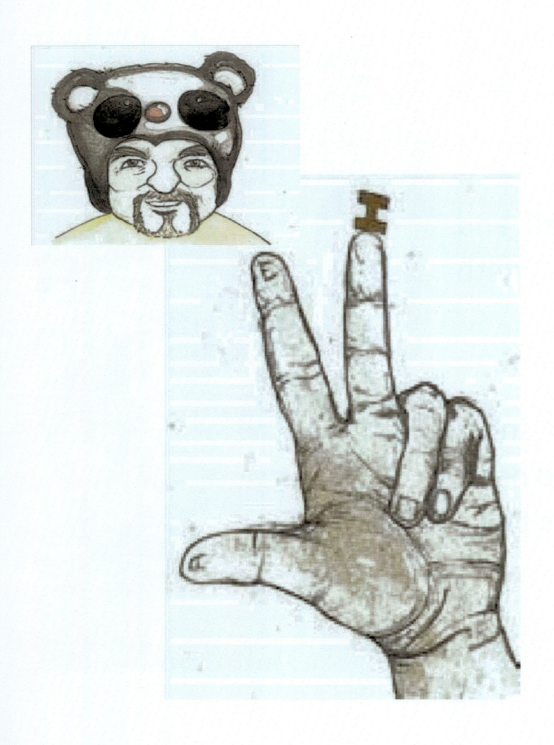

'I' is for **'indiVidual'** as in you or me but only one of us and no one else.

Big 'I' is tall and straight with a hat as well as a shoe.

Little 'i' is short and straight with the hat thrown above.

The vowel 'i' is a word by itself as in "I".

'**O**' is for '**o**ther', which is not you or me but somebody else.

'O' goes round and round whether big or little.

Where does it start and where does it stop
nobody knows.

The vowel 'o' is in three words "**hello to you**".

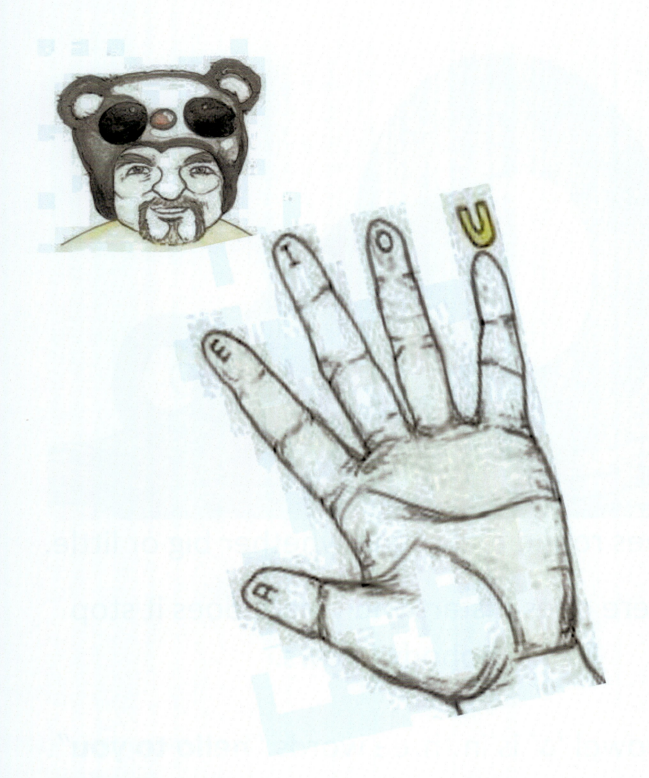

'U' is for 'us', meaning you and me together.

'U' is a happy smile; Big 'U' is a big smile and little "u" is a smaller smile.

The vowel 'u' is in the word "you".

Now we put all these words with the vowels together so, "I say hello to you" with a wave of the hand.

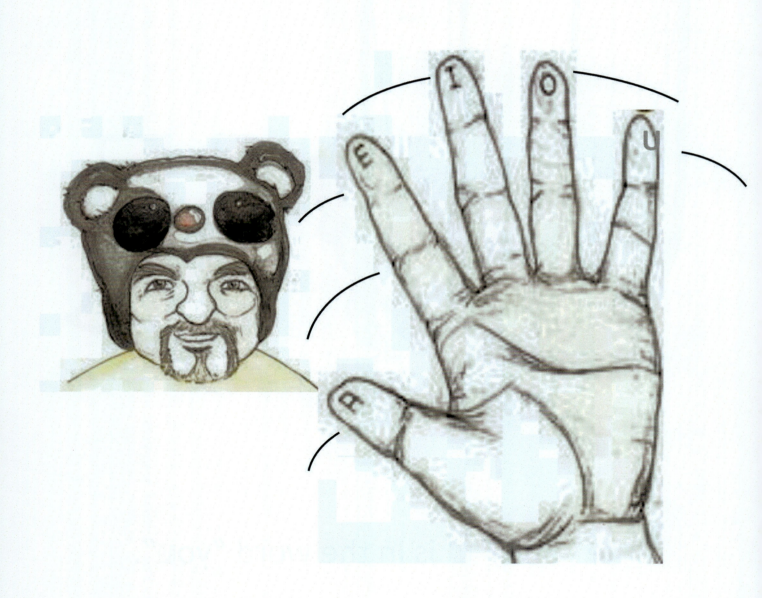

Now write your, family or friend's name and count how many vowels are in the name?

There are some words that have none of the 5 vowels but another letter instead!

Can you think of any?

I will give you a hint for one word that is something we see every day;

"It is always above you, can be blue or orange or pink or white or grey or even sometimes black.

It can be bright or dark, full of sparkles or puffs of white or birds or empty with nothing at all to see."

Can you guess what it is?

"Sky", did you guess it right?

This word does not have a, e, i, o or u but another instead.

It is the letter 'y' which is used instead of using one of the 5 vowels in some words.

Now let us think of more words that have the vowel 'a' in them.

C _ t

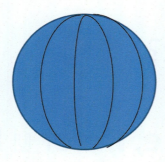

B _ ll

How many words can you think of that have the vowel 'e' in them?

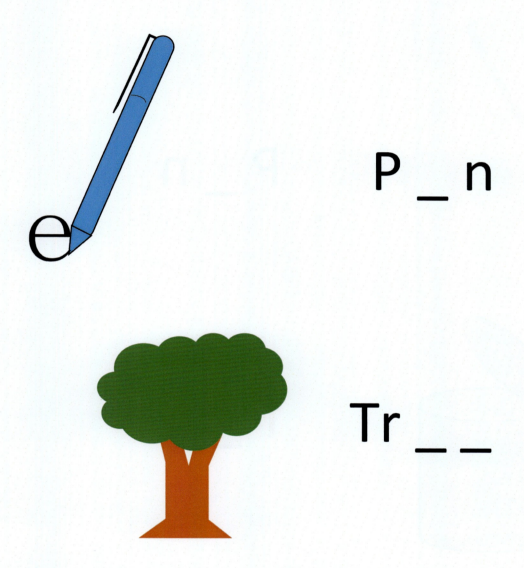

P _ n

Tr _ _

What about words that have the vowel 'i' in them?

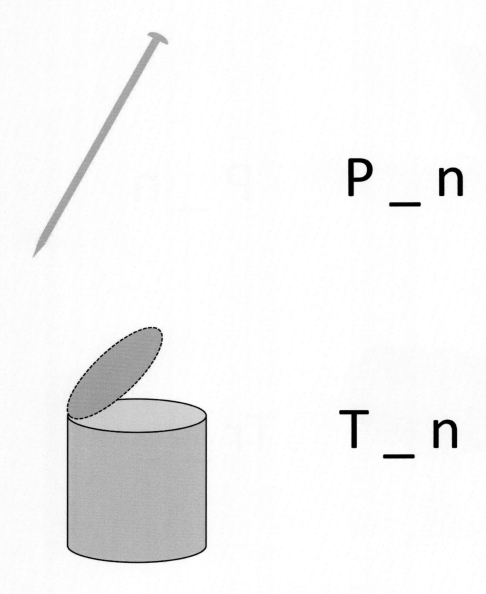

P _ n

T _ n

Do you know any other words that have the vowel 'o' in them?

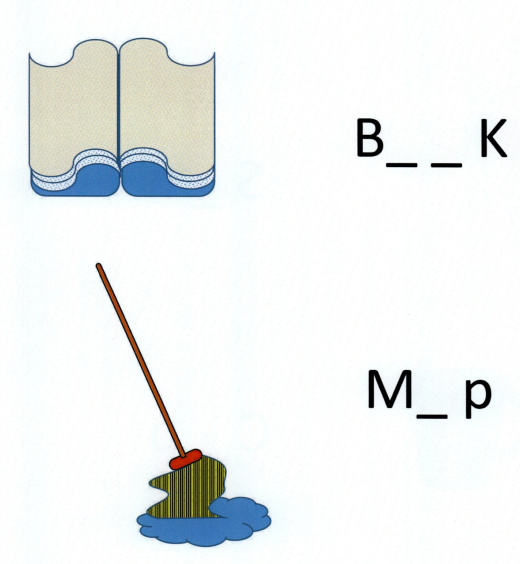

B _ _ K

M _ p

Do you know any other words that have the vowel 'u' in them?

S _ n

C _ p

Some words have no vowel but a 'y' in the word; do you know any?

Here is a hint; what is a word that you ask when you do not know?

It sounds just like the letter.

Printed in the United States
By Bookmasters